THE ODD SQUAD

BY ALLAN PLENDERLEITH

RAVETTE PUBLISHING

First published in 2001
Reprinted in 2002
Ravette Publishing Limited
Unit 3, Tristar Centre
Star Road, Partridge Green
West Sussex RH13 8RA

THE ODD SQUAD and all related characters
© 2001 by Allan Plenderleith
www.theoddsquad.co.uk

Printed in Malta by Gutenberg Press

ISBN: 1 84161 094 1

LIKE MANY
WOMEN, MAUDE
WAS DISMAYED
TO DISCOVER
HER BUM HAD
MOVED SOUTH.

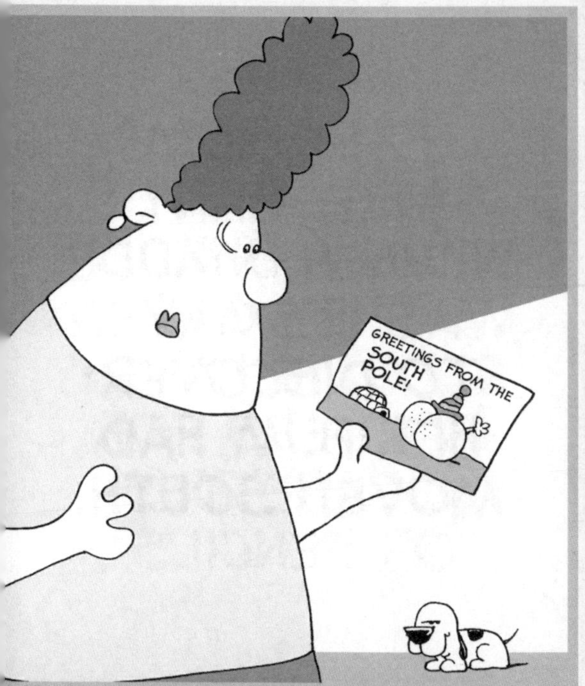
GREETINGS FROM THE
SOUTH POLE!

FAR FROM
SAGGY BOOBS
BEING A BURDEN,
THEY CAN
BECOME HANDY
HOLDERS FOR
CIGARETTES
OR PENCILS.

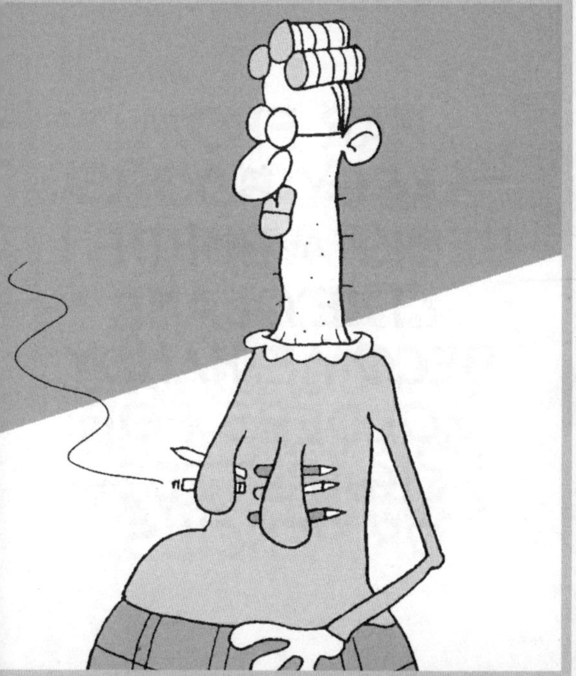

HAVING COVERED
HER MAN IN
CHOCOLATE
SAUCE, MAUDE
HAD GOT A BIT
CARRIED AWAY.

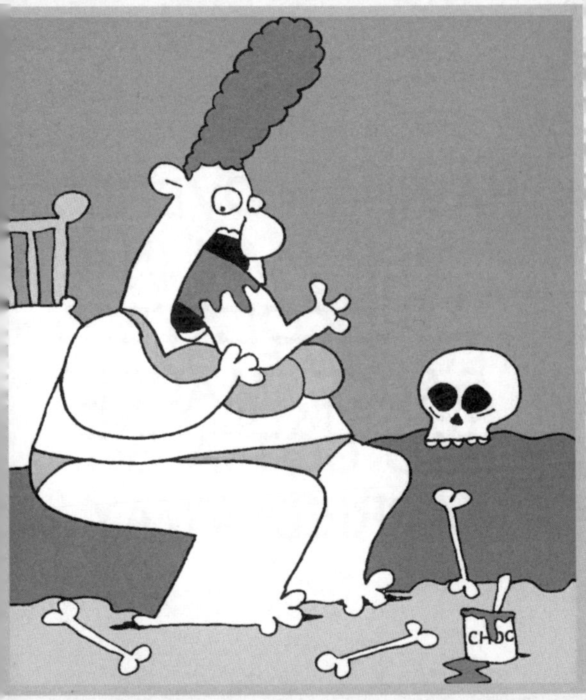
CHOC

MAUDE DECIDES
IT'S TIME TO DO
HER BIKINI LINE.

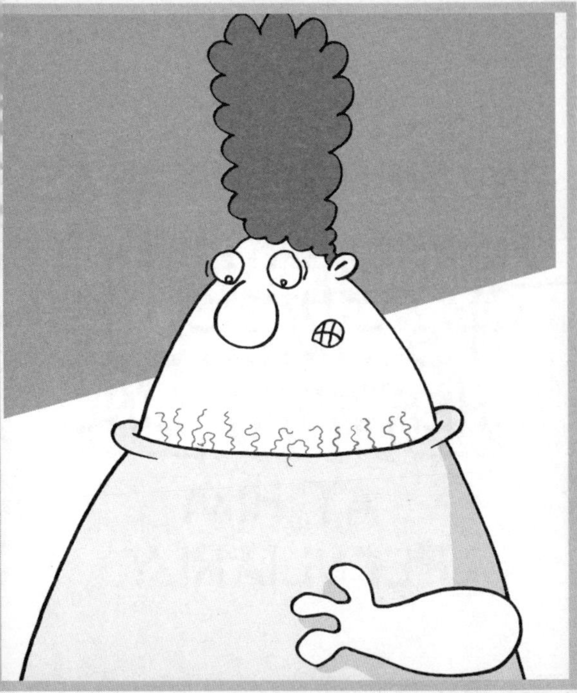

JEFF WAS WORRIED. IT WAS THE FOURTH DAY OF MAUDE'S DIET AND SHE HAD BEGUN TO LOOK AT HIM PECULIARLY.

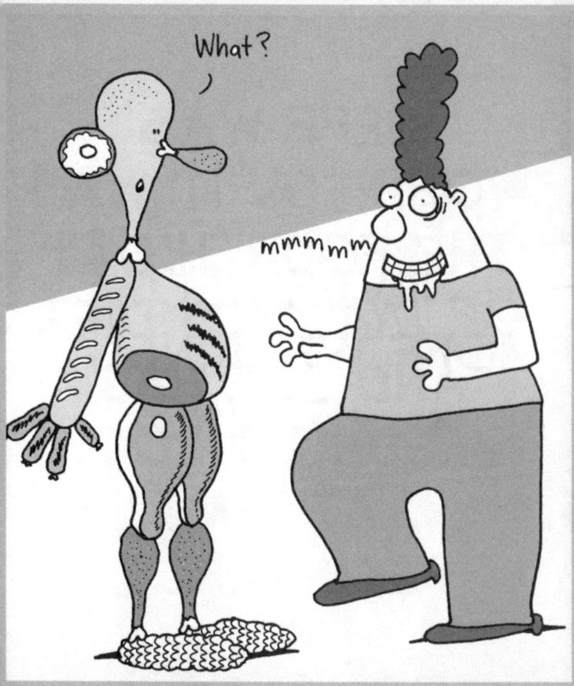
What?
mmmmmm

NEVER BLOW
OFF WEARING A
G-STRING.

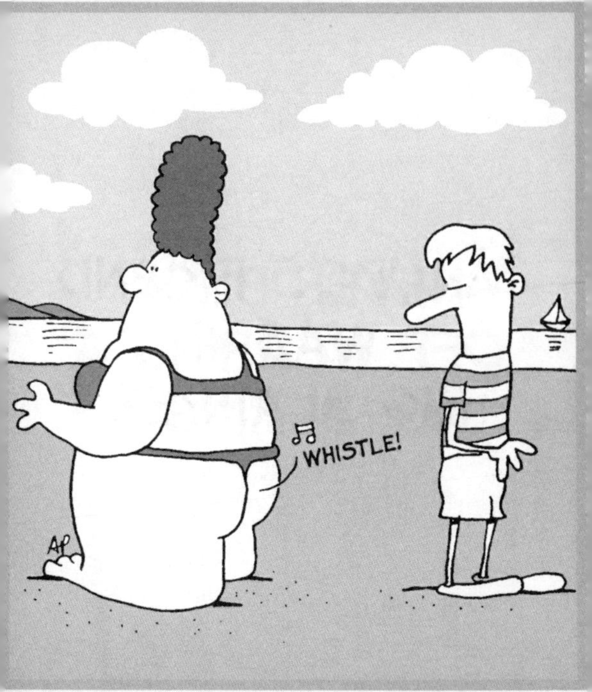
WHISTLE!
AP

MAUDE'S FRIEND
WAS A
BIG SLAPPER.

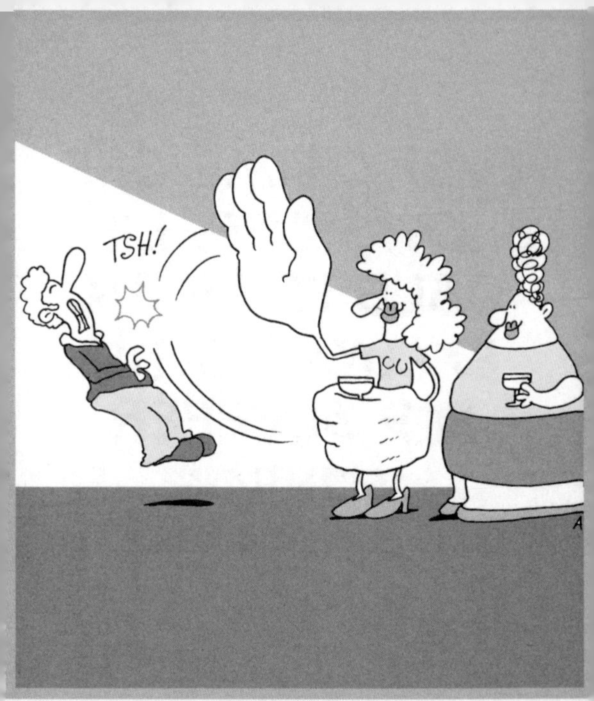
TSH!
CU

EVERY TIME SHE BLOWS OFF, LILY USES IT AS AN EXCUSE TO DO HER MARILYN MONROE IMPRESSION.

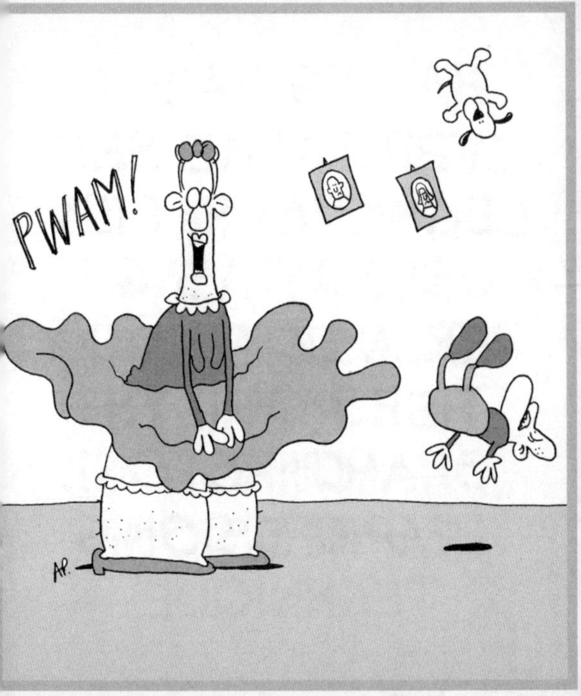
PWAM!
AP.

HAVING FAILED TO TALK THE BANK MANAGER INTO GIVING HER A LOAN, LILY TRIES OUT THE 'SHARON STONE LEG-CROSSING TECHNIQUE'.

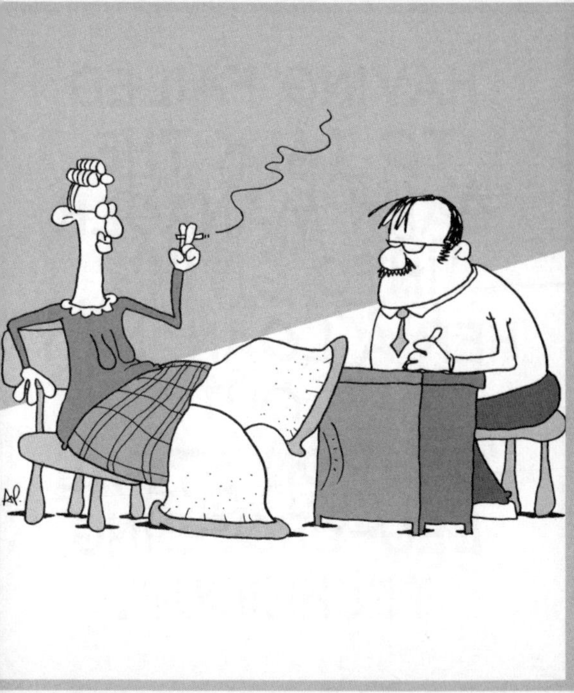

MAUDE MAKES USE OF THAT LEOPARD SKIN SKIRT SHE USED TO WEAR AS A TEENAGER.

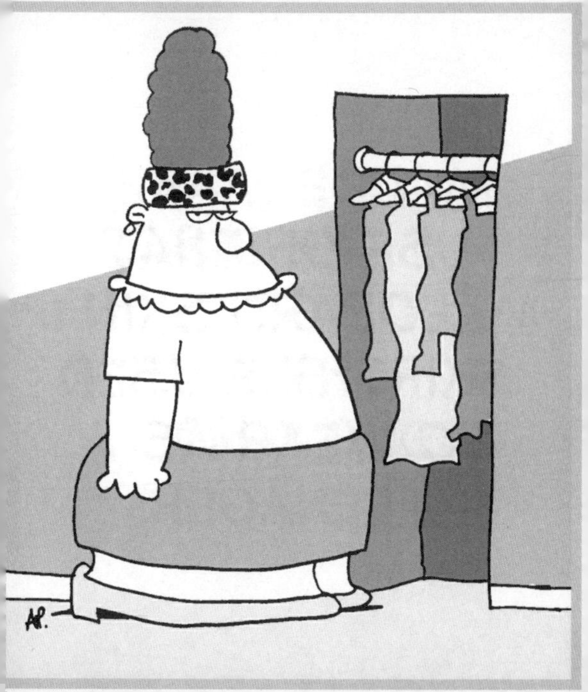
AP.

AT THE DISCO,
MAUDE GETS INTO
A FIGHT WITH A
DIRTY HOE.

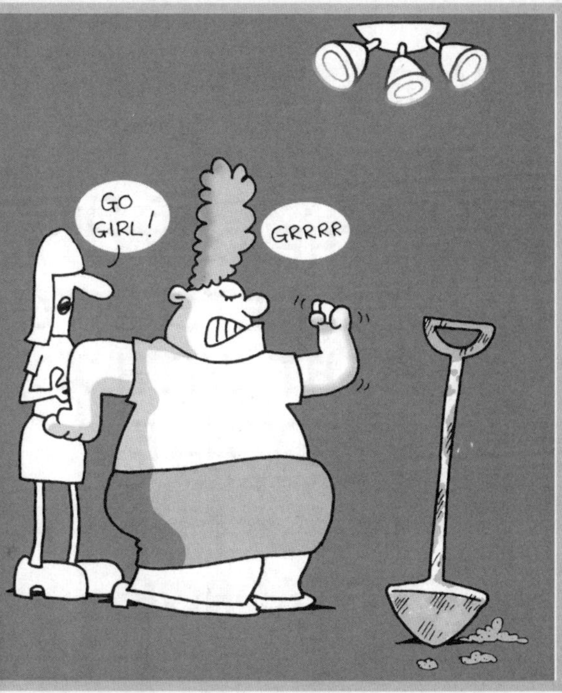
GO GIRL!
GRRRR

WHEN JEFF SAID
HE WANTED TO
GO 'INTO THE BIG
BROWN TUNNEL
OF LOVE' MAUDE
WAS RELIEVED TO
DISCOVER IT
WASN'T A
METAPHOR.

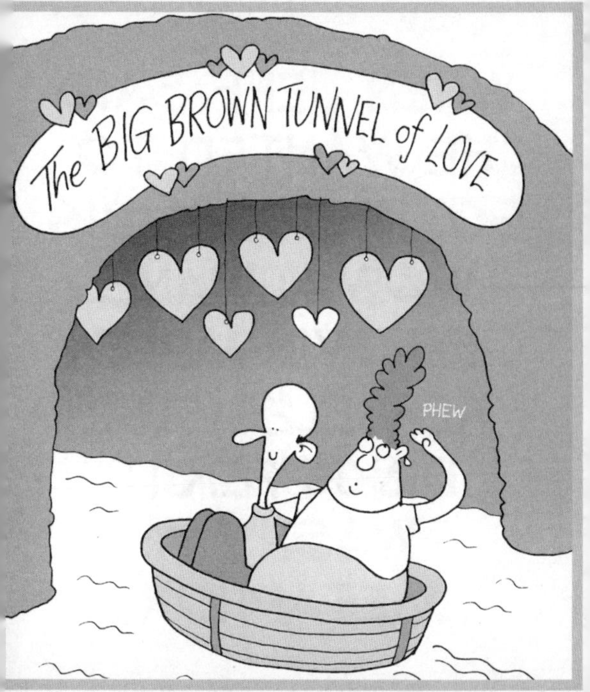
The BIG BROWN TUNNEL of LOVE
PHEW

MAUDE
WAS ALWAYS
SHOWING OFF
HER CLEAVAGE
IN PUBLIC.

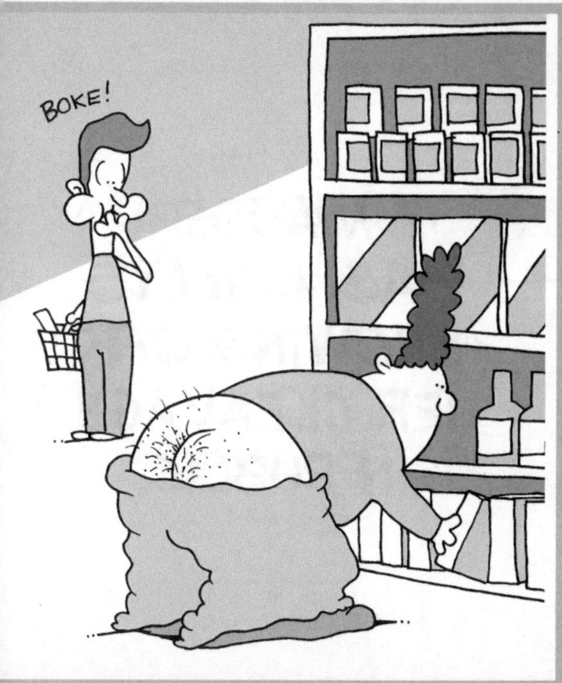
BOKE!

MAUDE AND
HER FRIEND
ALWAYS GO TO
THE TOILET IN
PEARS.

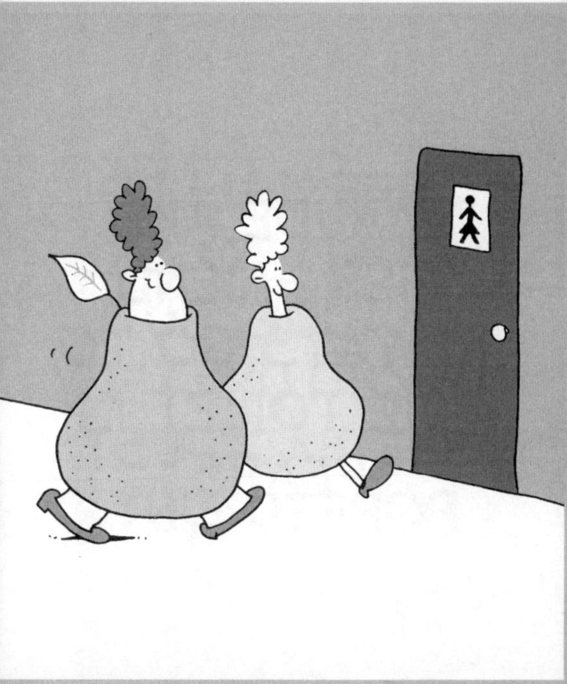

JEFF CALLED
ROUND TO SEE
MAUDE, BUT
UNFORTUNATELY
SHE HAD JUST
POPPED OUT.

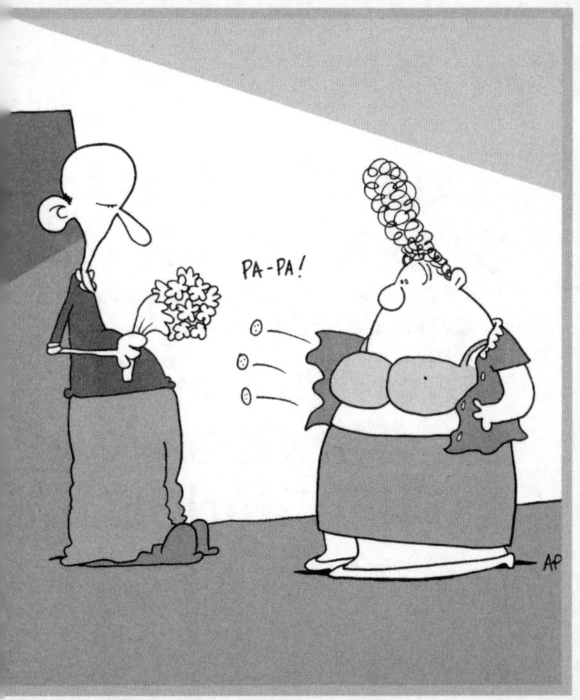
PA-PA!
AP

ALF KNEW TO
STEER CLEAR OF
LILY, BECAUSE
SHE WAS GOING
THROUGH
'THE CHANGE'.

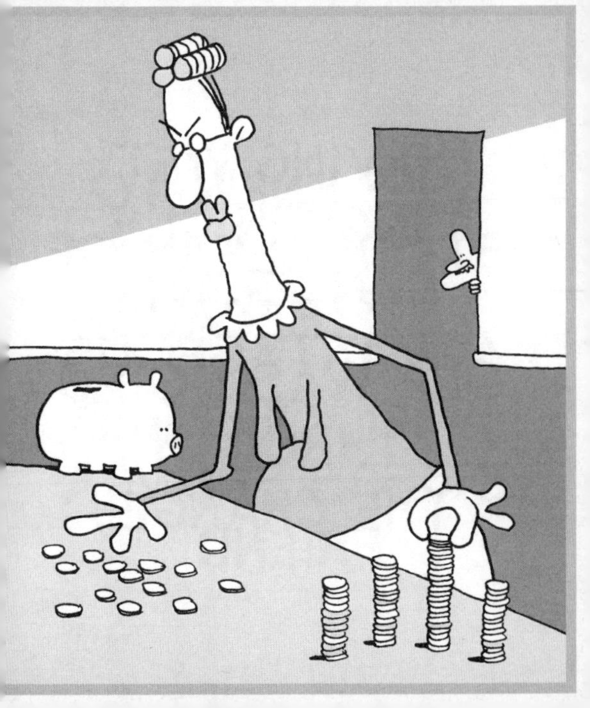

HAVING WET FINGERNAILS CAN PROVE ADVANTAGEOUS WHEN OFFERED CRISPS FROM A FRIEND.

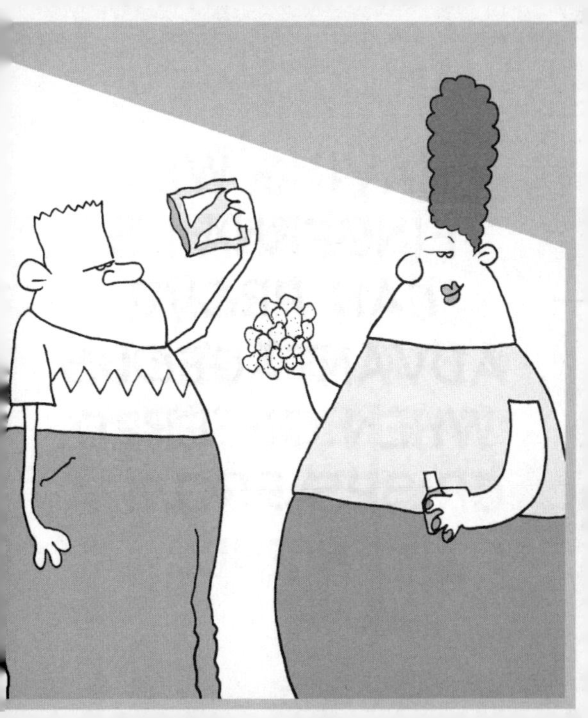

MAUDE
HAD HEARD
BOOB TUBES
WERE IN THIS
SEASON.

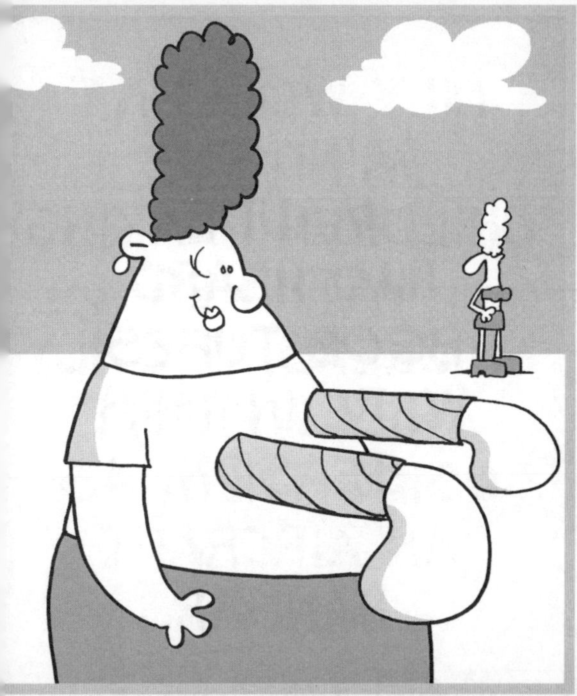

LILY WOULDN'T MIND THE CHILDREN PLAYING WITH HER KNICKERS, IF ONLY THEY WEREN'T USING THEM AS AN AIRCRAFT HANGAR.

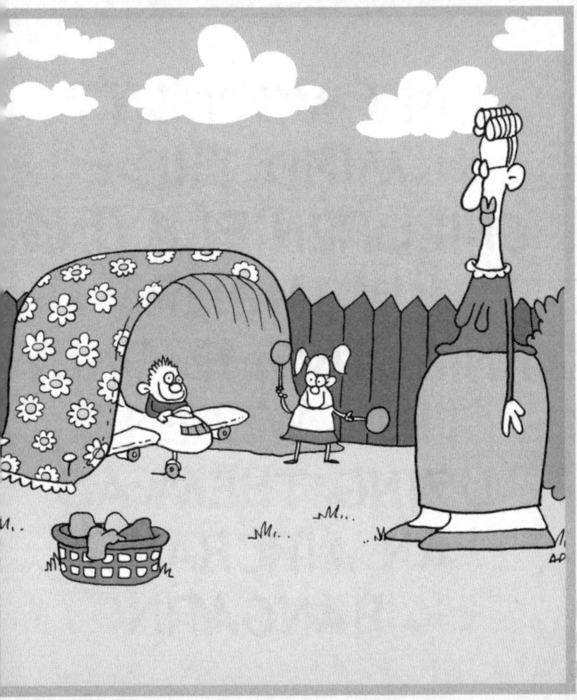

APPARENTLY
NO-ONE ELSE
COULD HEAR IT,
BUT MAUDE
COULD.
THE CAKE WAS
WHISPERING:
'LICK MY ICING',
'LICK MY ICING'.

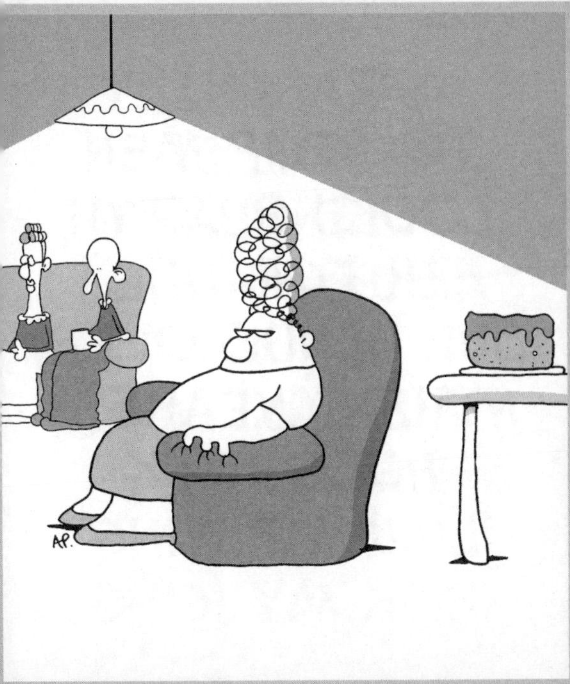
AP.

TO STOP MEN
LOOKING DOWN
HER TOP WHEN
SHE BENDS OVER,
MAUDE WEARS A
POLO NECK
JUMPER.

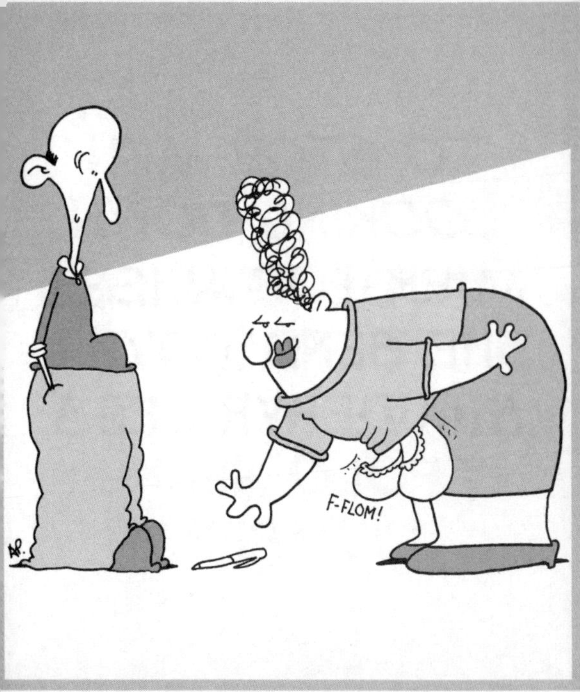
F-FLOM!

MAUDE REALISES
IT'S TIME TO
SHAVE HER LEGS.

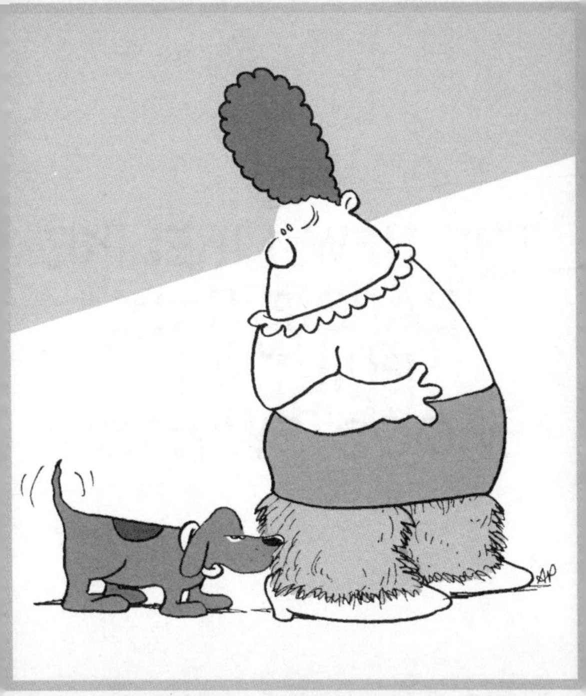

THE NEW LIFELIKE
BARBIE HAS
BUILT-IN
MOOD SWINGS.

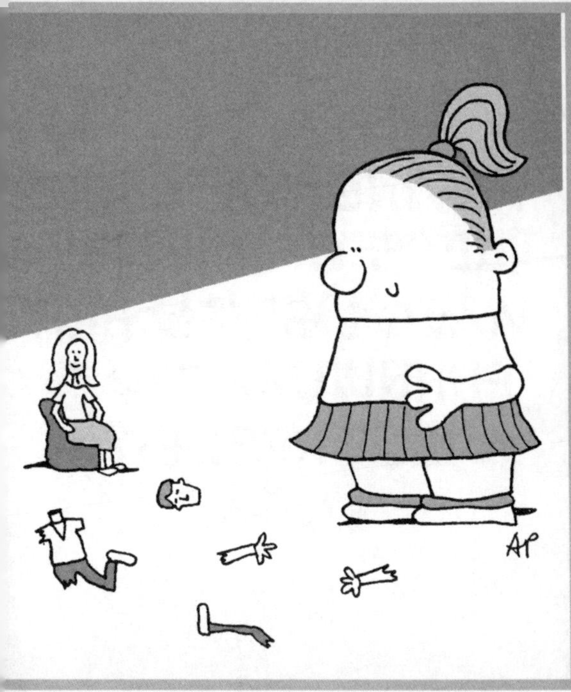

HAVING WATCHED
LOTS OF DIY TV,
MAUDE GIVES HER
FURNITURE THAT
'DISTRESSED'
LOOK.

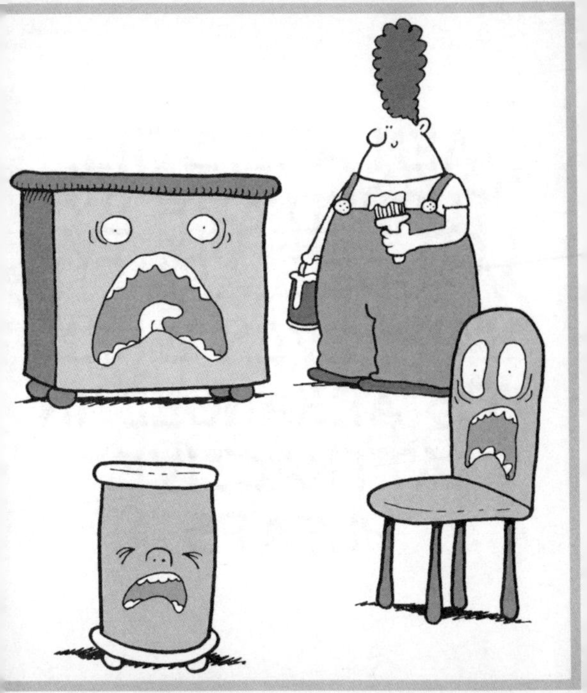

MEN ARE STILL TURNED OFF BY MAUDE'S ARMPIT HAIR, EVEN WHEN IT'S ARRANGED IN ATTRACTIVE PLEATS.

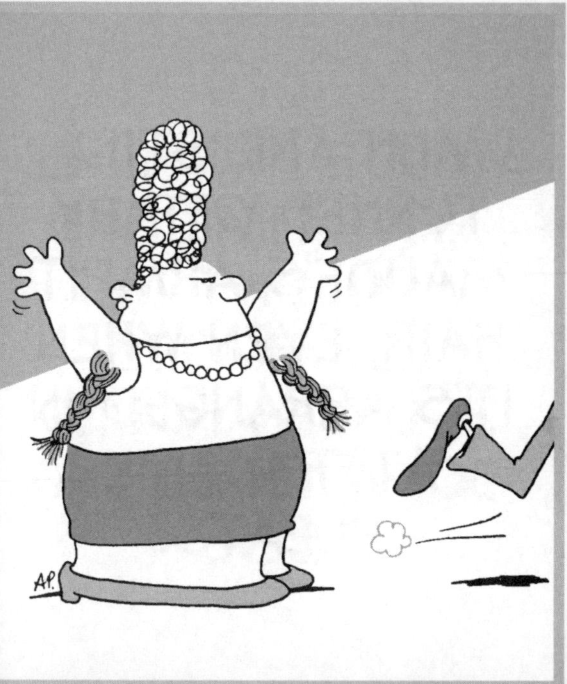
AP.

MAUDE PROMISED NEXT TIME SHE WOULDN'T LET HER BOOBS BOUNCE AROUND SO MUCH DURING SEX.

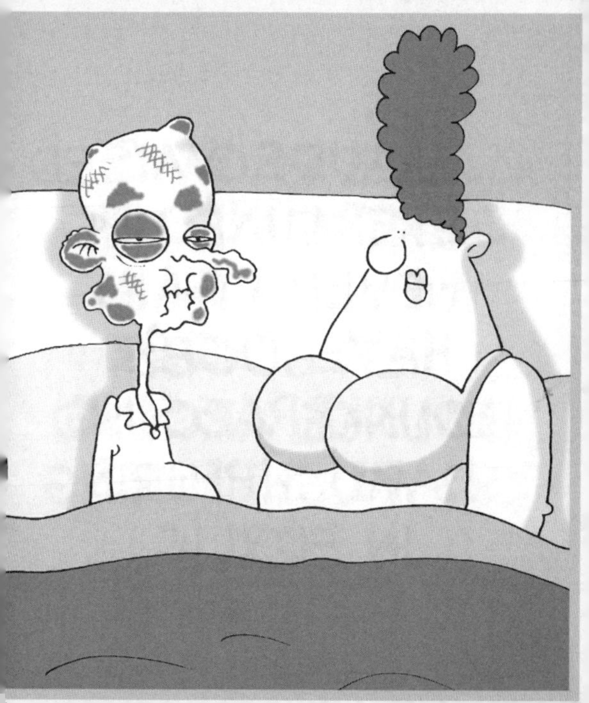

MAUDE WAS
DETERMINED TO
NEVER AGAIN
HAVE THOSE
EMBARRASSING
HARD NIPPLES
IN PUBLIC.

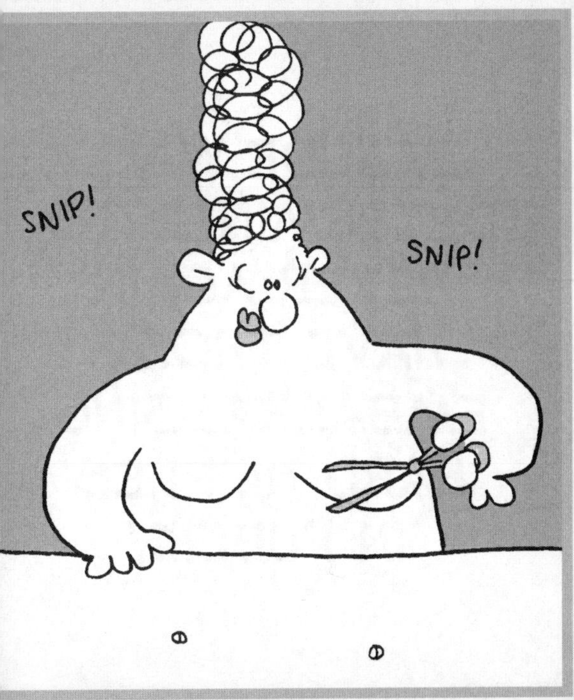
SNIP!
SNIP!

USING SOME LIPSTICK ON HER DOUBLE CHIN, LILY LIKES TO SCARE THE CHILDREN WITH HER 'EXTRA MOUTH' ROUTINE.

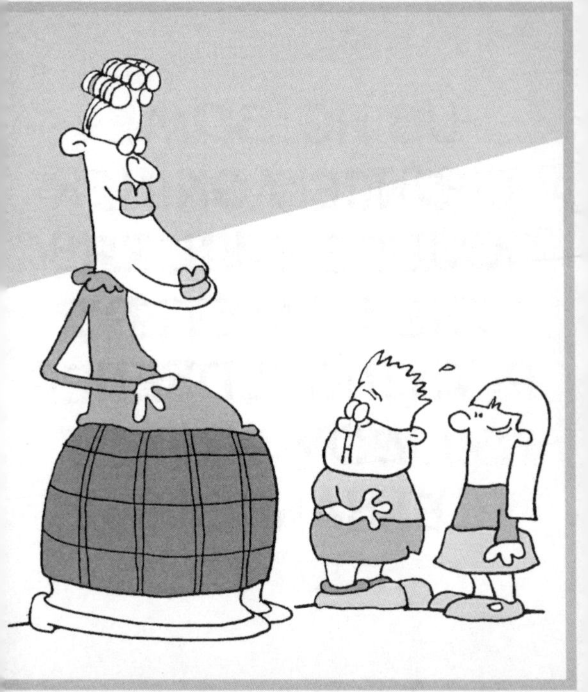

ONCE AGAIN,
MAUDE CATCHES
THE HAMSTERS
PLAYING WITH HER
SILICON BREAST
ENHANCERS.

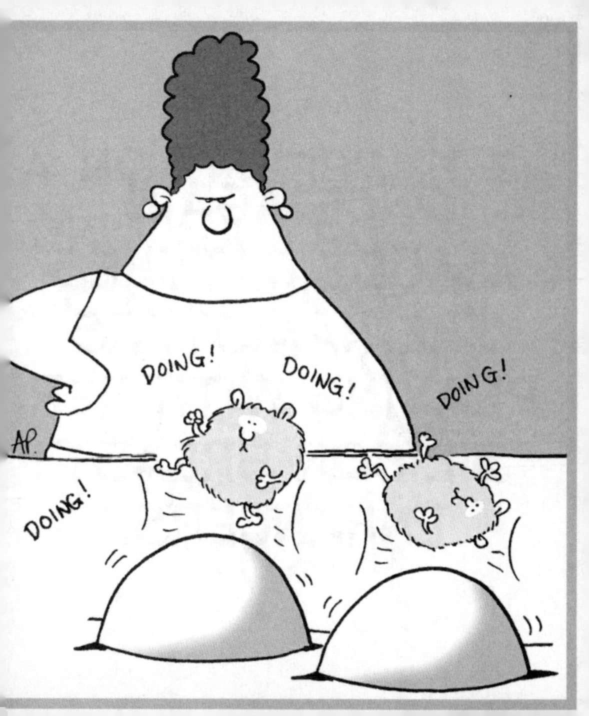
DOING!
DOING!
DOING!
DOING!
AP.

IT HAPPENED ON A TUESDAY AROUND 12 NOON: LILY'S BODY FINALLY GAVE UP ITS BATTLE WITH GRAVITY.

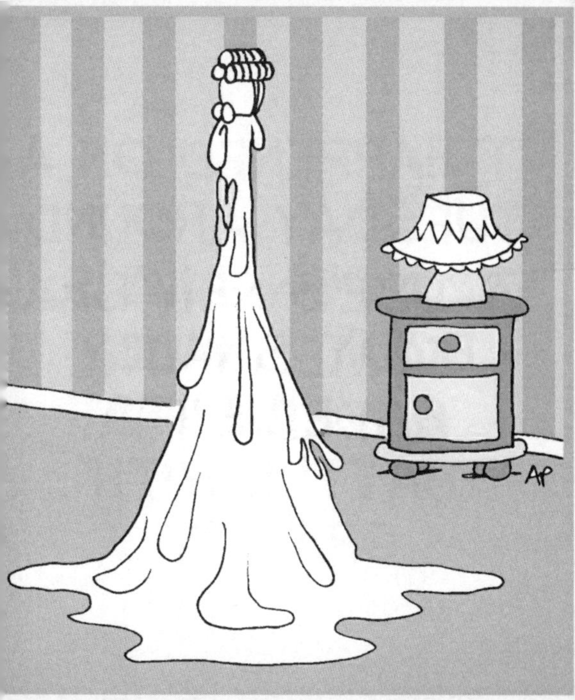
AP

MAUDE'S NEW BRA
COMES WITH
'ADDED LIFT'.

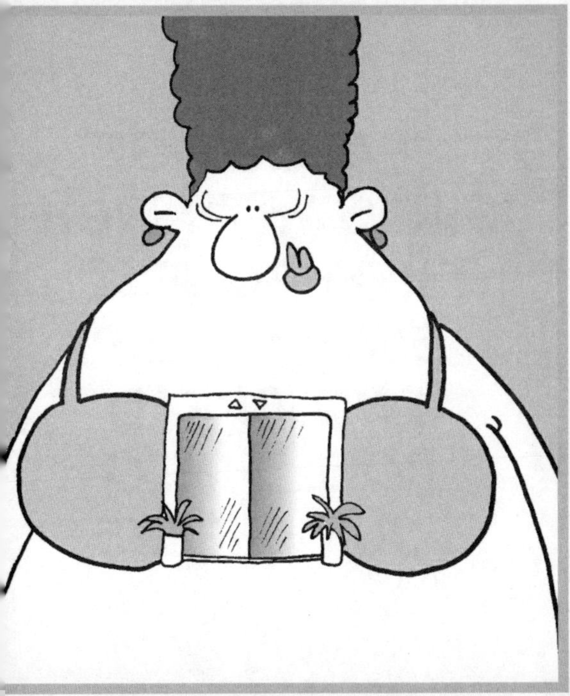

JEALOUS OF GIRLS WITH HIGH CHEEKBONES? SIMPLY SLIP TWO BREAD ROLLS INTO YOUR CHEEKS.

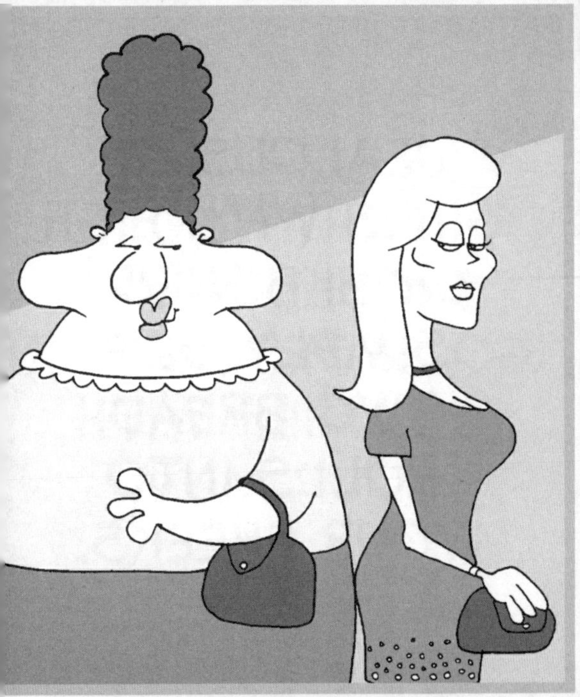

WHY YOU SHOULD NEVER GO SHOPPING FOR CLOTHES WITH YOUR MUM.

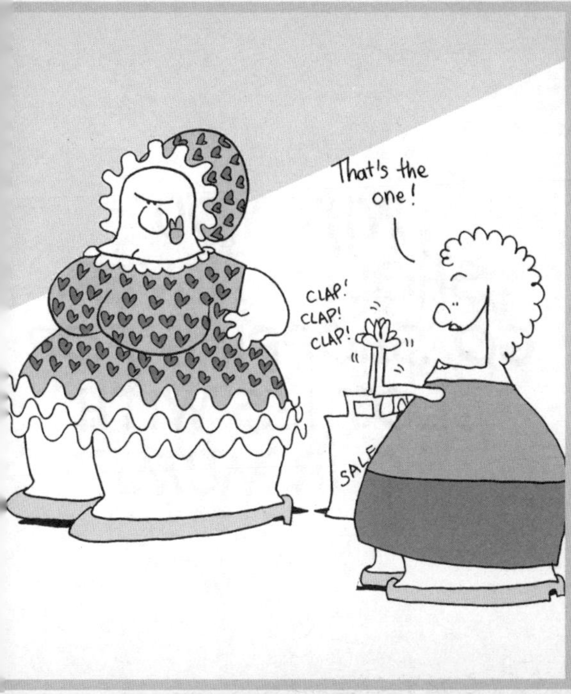
That's the one!
CLAP!
CLAP!
CLAP!
SALE

JANICE WAS WRONG. MAUDE COULD STILL GET INTO A SIZE 12.

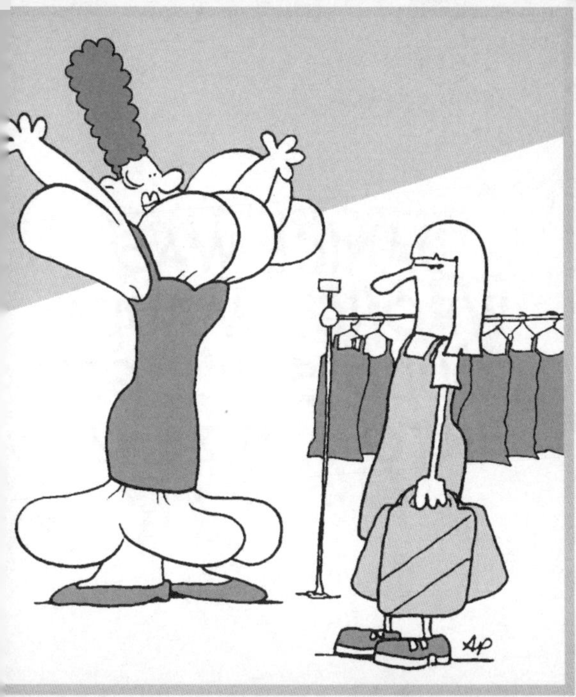

BEFORE THEY GO OUT, MAUDE AND HER FRIEND LIKE TO GET TANKED UP.

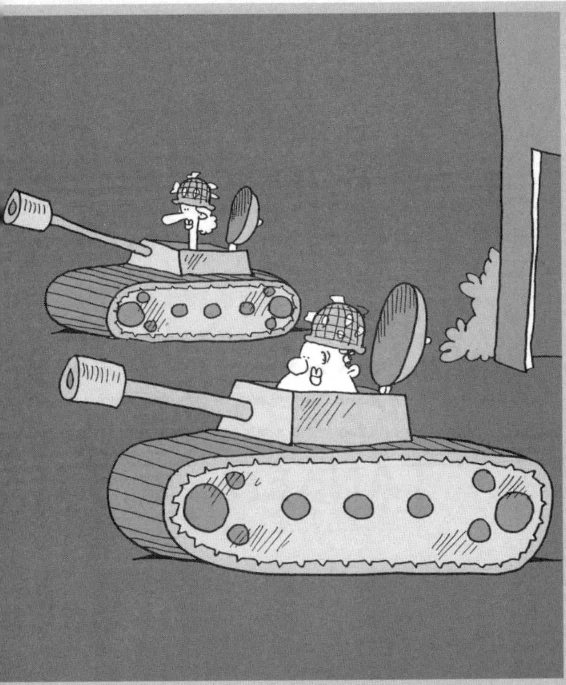

IF SHE GOES TOO FAST WHILST RIDING HER BIKE, LILY EXPERIENCES 'SEVERE BOOB FLAPPAGE'.

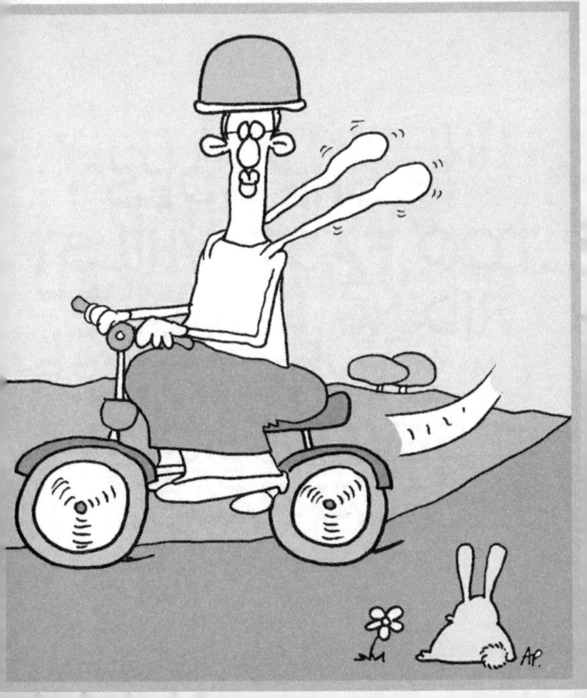
AP.

UNFORTUNATELY, MAUDE HAD ACTUALLY ASKED THE PLASTIC SURGEON TO TAKE 'YEARS' OFF HER.

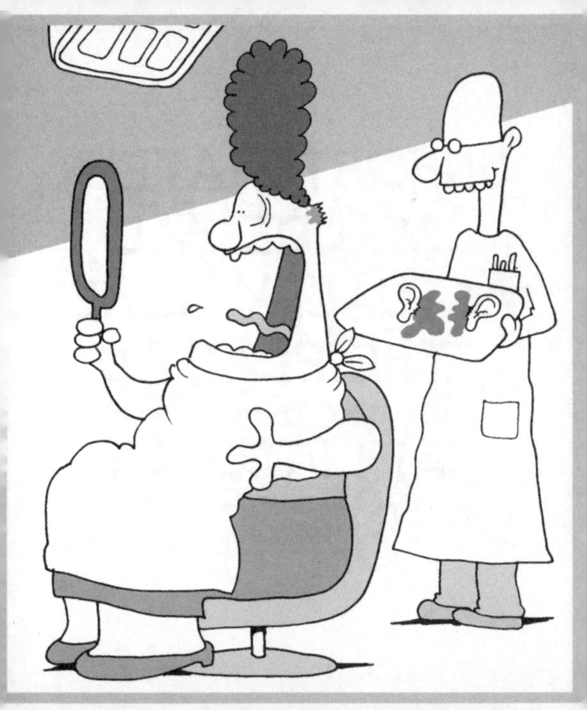

AS A CHEAP
ALTERNATIVE TO
A FACE LIFT,
LILY TIES HER
HAIR INTO AN
OVERTIGHT BUN.

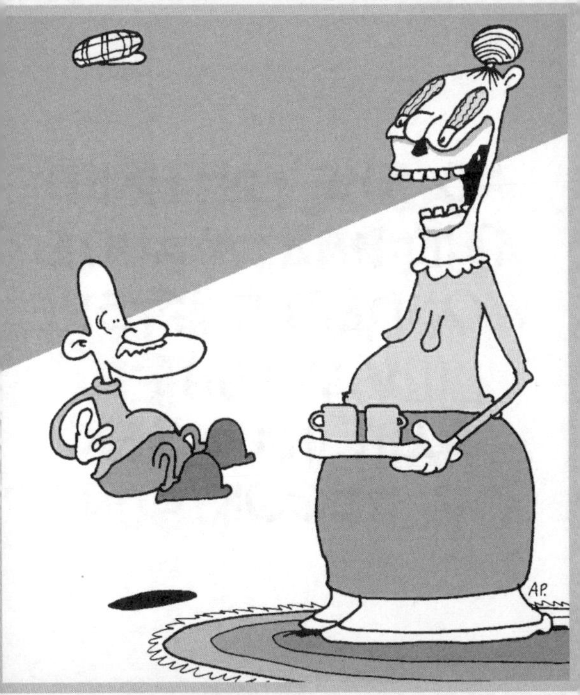
AP.

AS SHE ENTERED
THE BAR, MAUDE
WONDERED IF SHE
HAD THAT
'JUST HAD SEX'
LOOK.

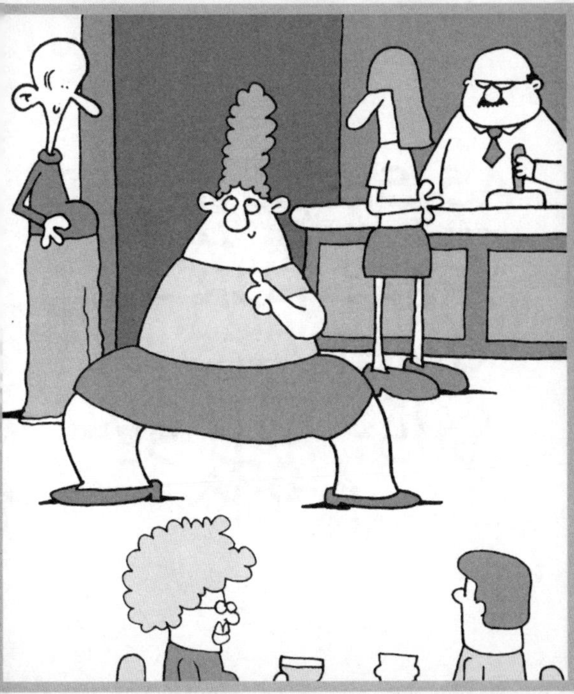

AS A SPECIAL
TREAT FOR ALF,
SOMETIMES LILY
GOES WITHOUT
A BRA.

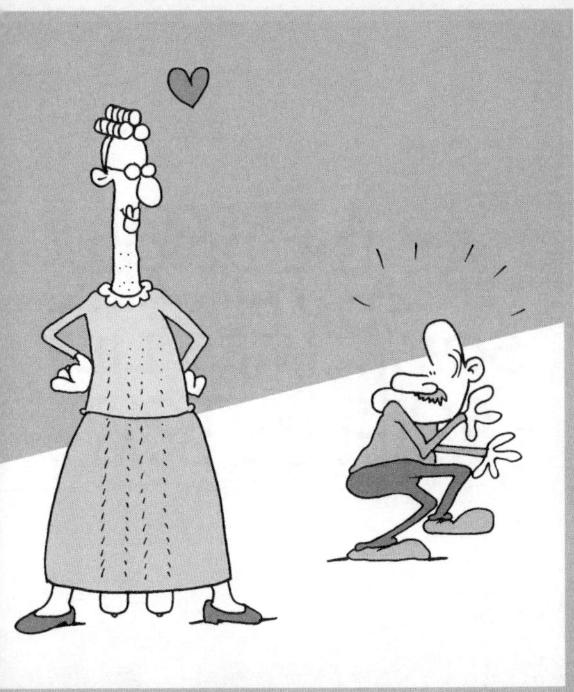

AT THE DISCO,
SOMEONE
PINCHED
MAUDE'S BUM.

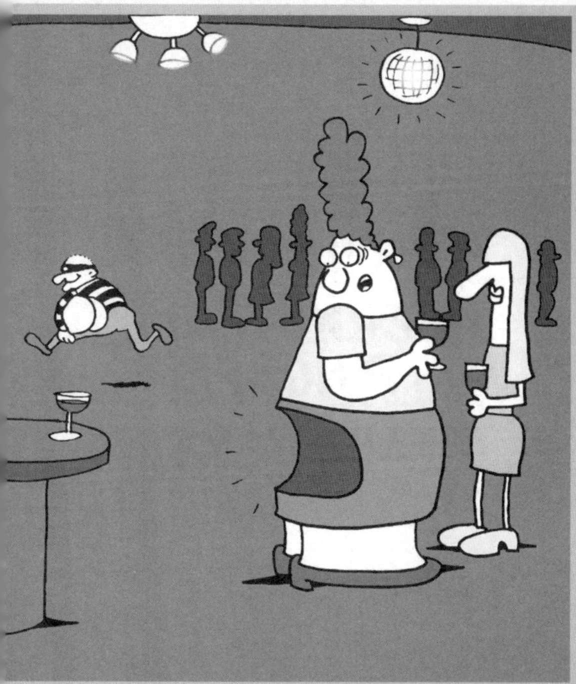

LILY
ACCIDENTALLY
WALKS OVER AN
AIR VENT.

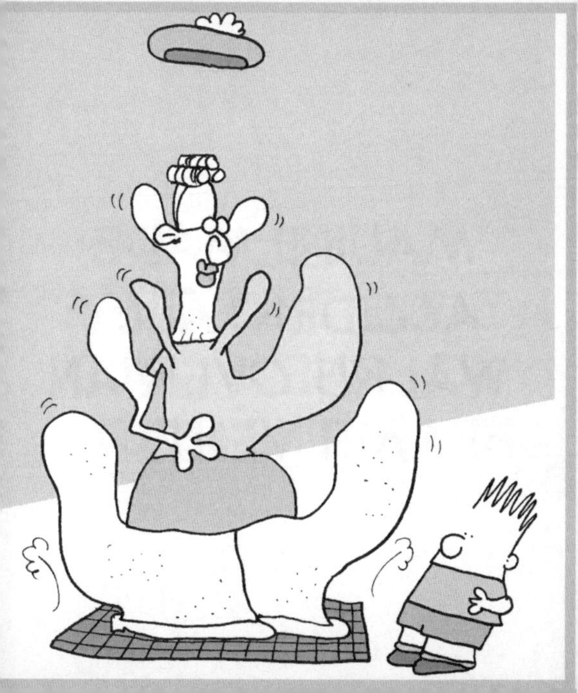

MAUDE MADE
SURE THIS TIME
NO-ONE WOULD
HEAR 'THE PLOP'.

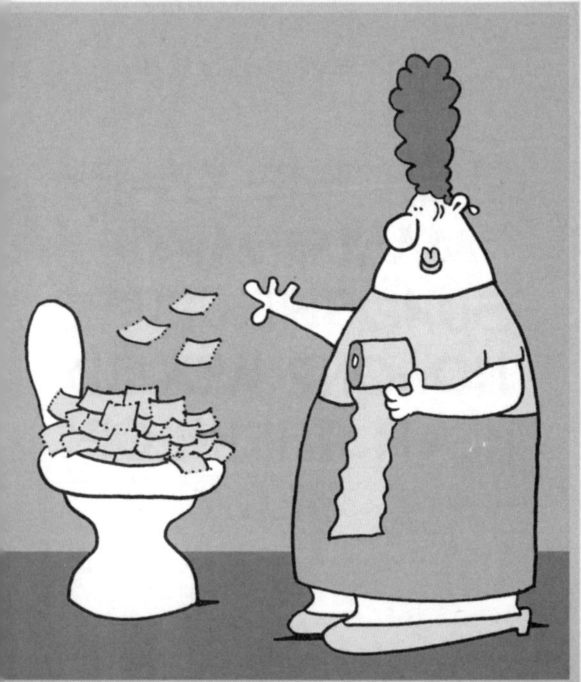

OVER THE YEARS,
MAUDE HAS
TAUGHT JEFF
HOW TO REALLY
SATISFY HER IN
BED.

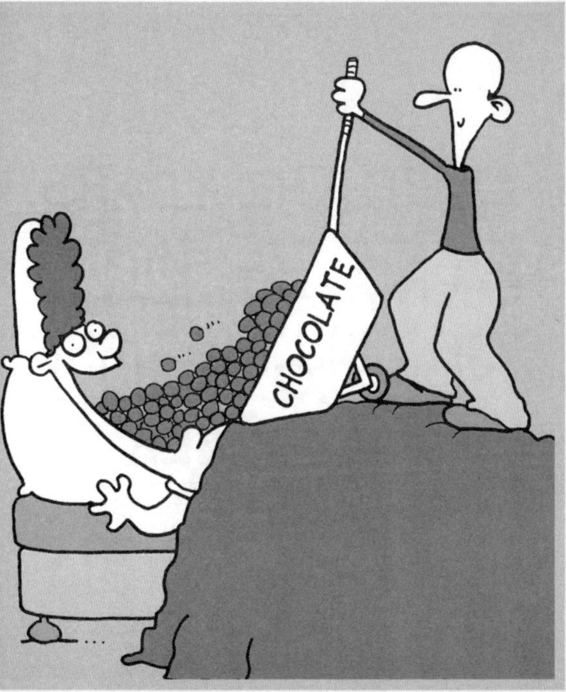
CHOCOLATE

MAUDE HAD HER OWN SUBTLE WAY OF TELLING JEFF SHE WAS IN THE MOOD.

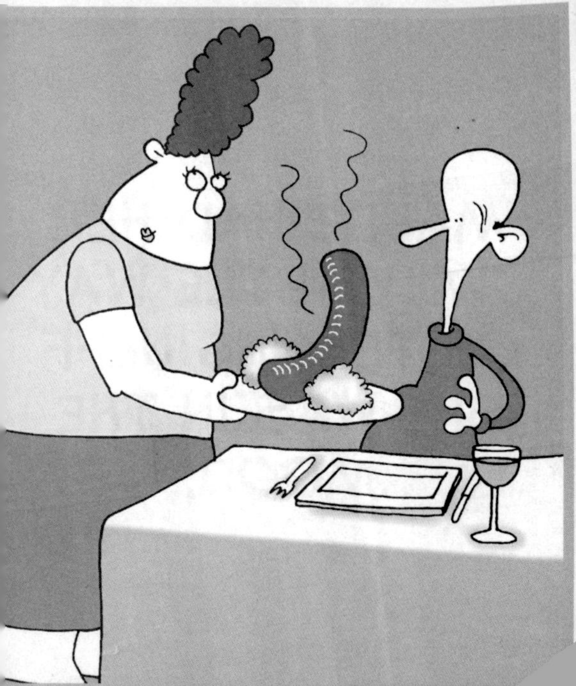

NEVER CROSS
A PARK IN
HIGH HEELS.